In the Footsteps of Explorers

Jacques Cartier

Exploring the St. Lawrence River

Jennifer Lackey

Crabtree Publishing Company

www.crabtreebooks.com

Crabtree Publishing Company
www.crabtreebooks.com

For Jeff, whose stories of the Cartier Precision Chewing Beavers kept me amused even though they didn't make it into the book, with thanks to Ellen for the opportunity.

Coordinating editor: Ellen Rodger
Series editor: Carrie Gleason
Project editor: Rachel Eagen
Editors: Adrianna Morganelli, L. Michelle Nielsen
Design and production coordinator: Rosie Gowsell
Cover design and production assistance: Samara Parent
Art direction: Rob MacGregor
Scanning technician: Arlene Arch-Wilson
Photo research: Allison Napier

Consultant: Stacy Hasselbacher, Museum Educator, The Mariners' Museum, Newport News, Virginia

Photo Credits: Bibliotheque Nationale, Paris, France, Giraudon/The Bridgeman Art Library International: p. 24; Musee Conde, Chantilly, France/The Bridgeman Art Library International: p. 9; Private Collection, Giraudon/The Bridgeman Art Library International: pp. 8-9; Private Collection, Index/The Bridgeman Art Library International: p. 6 (top); Private Collection, Peter Newark American Pictures/The Bridgeman Art Library International: p. 26 (bottom left); Richard Cummins/Corbis: p. 29 (left); John Heseltine/Corbis: p. 30; The Granger Collection, New York: cover, pp. 4-5, pp. 10-11, p. 27; Donald Gargano/istock International: p. 23 (middle left); Pierrette Guertin/istock International: p. 23 (middle right); Laurie Knight/istock International: p. 20 (bottom left); Kevin Russ/istock International: p. 26 (bottom right); Micha Strzelecki/istock International: p. 6 (bottom right); Brian Wilcox/istock International: p. 6 (bottom left); Don Wilkie/istock International: p. 20 (top right); Nancy Carter/North Wind Picture Archives: p. 12 (bottom right); North Wind Picture Archive: p. 8, p. 13, p. 14, p. 15, pp. 16-17, p. 19 (top), p. 21, p. 28, p. 31(top); George Bernard/Photo Researchers, Inc.: p. 10; Biophoto Associates/Photo Researchers, Inc.: p. 22; Mark Harmel/Photo Researchers, Inc.: p. 25; Other images from stock photo cd.

Illustrations: Lauren Fast: p. 4; David Wysotski: pp. 22-23

Cartography: Jim Chernishenko: title page, p. 18

Cover: Jacques Cartier came to North America with several different goals in mind. He did not find what he was looking for, but he did explore regions that the French would later settle.

Title page: Cartier's voyages to North America helped the French to establish the large French territory of New France.

Sidebar icon: Cartier and his crew learned to make a vitamin-rich tea by boiling the bark and leaves of spruce trees. This recipe was used to cure and prevent scurvy, a common seafaring illness.

Library and Archives Canada Cataloguing in Publication

Lackey, Jennifer D. B., 1969-
    Jacques Cartier : exploring the St. Lawrence River / Jennifer Lackey.

(In the footsteps of explorers)
Includes index.
ISBN-13: 978-0-7787-2430-8 (bound)
ISBN-10: 0-7787-2430-1 (bound)
ISBN-13: 978-0-7787-2466-7 (pbk)
ISBN-10: 0-7787-2466-2 (pbk)

    1. Cartier, Jacques, 1491-1557--Juvenile literature. 2. Explorers--France--Biography--Juvenile literature. 3. Explorers--America--Biography--Juvenile literature. 4. Saint Lawrence River--Discovery and exploration. 5. Canada--Discovery and exploration--French--Juvenile literature. I. Title. II. Series.

FC301.C37L32 2006   j971.01'13092   C2006-902144-9

Library of Congress Cataloging-in-Publication Data

Lackey, Jennifer, 1969-
  Jacques Cartier : exploring the St. Lawrence River / written by Jennifer Lackey.
      p. cm. -- (In the footsteps of explorers)
  Includes index.
  ISBN-13: 978-0-7787-2430-8 (rlb)
  ISBN-10: 0-7787-2430-1 (rlb)
  ISBN-13: 978-0-7787-2466-7 (pbk)
  ISBN-10: 0-7787-2466-2 (pbk)
  1. Cartier, Jacques, 1491-1557--Juvenile literature. 2. Explorers--America--Biography--Juvenile literature. 3. Explorers--Saint Lawrence River--Biography--Juvenile literature. 4. Explorers--France--Biography--Juvenile literature. 5. Saint Lawrence River--Discovery and exploration--Juvenile literature. 6. Canada--Discovery and exploration--Juvenile literature. 7. Canada--History--To 1763 (New France)--Juvenile literature. I. Title. II. Series.
  E133.C3L34 2006
  971.01'13092--dc22
  [B]   2006012401

Crabtree Publishing Company
www.crabtreebooks.com   1-800-387-7650

Published in Canada
Crabtree Publishing
616 Welland Ave.
St. Catharines, Ontario
L2M 5V6

Published in the United States
Crabtree Publishing
PMB16A
350 Fifth Ave., Suite 3308
New York, NY 10118

Published in the United Kingdom
Crabtree Publishing
White Cross Mills
High Town, Lancaster
LA1 4XS

Published in Australia
Crabtree Publishing
386 Mt. Alexander Rd.
Ascot Vale (Melbourne)
VIC 3032

Contents

A Northern Beginning

Jacques Cartier was the first European to explore the Gulf of St. Lawrence, the St. Lawrence River, and the land that bordered these waterways. Cartier's expeditions led to the building of French settlements at the present-day cities of Montreal and Quebec City in Canada.

Changing Vision

The king of France, Francois I, sent Cartier on three voyages, each with a different goal. Cartier's first assignment was to discover the Northwest Passage, a sea route that Europeans believed would lead to Asia and the valuable trade goods there. By the second voyage, Cartier was looking for riches in the legendary kingdom of Saguenay, which the local Native peoples told him lay in the northern regions of present-day Canada. On the third trip, Cartier was part of a large expedition to start a French colony.

(left) Cartier never found what he was looking for, but his expeditions paved the way for other French successes in present-day Canada.

(background) An illustration of Jacques Cartier and fellow settlers landing at Labrador, in Newfoundland, in 1541.

New Lands, New Species

When Europeans explored other parts of the world, they encountered many different kinds of animals and plants that they had never seen before. The following is a passage from Cartier's account of one of his voyages, in which his crew saw a polar bear for the first time in the sea around present-day Funk Island off the coast of Newfoundland. Cartier called this island *Isle des Oiseaux*, or Island of Birds.

"Notwithstanding that the island lies fourteen leagues from shore, bears swim out to it from the mainland in order to feed on these birds; and our men found one as big as a calf and as white as a swan that sprang into the sea in front of them. And the next day...on continuing our voyage in the direction of the mainland, we caught sight of this bear about halfway, swimming towards land as fast as we were sailing; and on coming up with him we gave chase with our long-boats and captured him by main force. His flesh was as good to eat as that of a two-year-old heifer [cow]."

Polar bears are adapted to the icy waters of northern Canada.

-1491-
Jacques Cartier is born in St. Malo, France.

-April 20, 1534-
Cartier departs St. Malo for his first voyage.

-May 19, 1535-
Cartier sets sail on his second voyage.

-May 23, 1541-
Cartier's third voyage begins.

-September 1, 1557-
Cartier dies.

The Age of Discovery

For thousands of years before Cartier was born, European merchants **had traded for valuable goods from the** Far East**,** such as spices, silk, and gold. The goods were traded along overland routes so that by the time they reached Europe, they were very expensive.

The Northwest Passage

In the late 1400s, Europeans began to look for new routes to the riches of Asia. In 1498, Portuguese explorer Vasco da Gama **navigated** a sea route from Europe to India by going around the southern tip of Africa. The Portuguese then set up trading posts in Africa, China, India, and the Moluccas, or Spice Islands. They eventually dominated European trade by attacking other merchant ships that tried to use their trade routes or stop at their trading posts. European navigators instead looked westward to where they believed a sea route to Asia existed. This route was called the Northwest Passage. By the time of Cartier's first expedition, many European nations, including England, Holland, and France, were exploring the Atlantic in a race to find the Northwest Passage.

(above) Vasco da Gama traveled to India by sailing around the southern tip of Africa.

(left) European merchants traveled far and wide for spices and minerals, such as pepper from the Moluccas, and salt from Africa.

An Impossible Task

No one knew at this time that finding the Northwest Passage was nearly an impossible task. Many European nations sponsored voyages to look for the Northwest Passage. Their expeditions increased European knowledge about the world and allowed them to build colonies in the lands they discovered, but the Northwest Passage was not navigated until Norwegian explorer Roald Amundsen's expedition in 1906. It took him three years to navigate the route. Even if early European explorers had found the Northwest Passage, it would not have been a useful route to Asia because it is frequently blocked by ice.

(background) Many explorers tried to navigate a route through North America to Asia, but most were forced back by harsh winter storms.

A Whole New World

Christopher Columbus changed the course of European exploration when he led an expedition in 1492. He was hoping to find a westward route to China, but instead found the islands of the Caribbean. Europeans saw great opportunities in what they referred to as the **New World**, including fertile land for colonies, and access to many valuable trade goods, such as animal furs, exotic fruits, and even gold. Many European nations rushed to the New World to stake their own claims on this exciting new frontier.

-1472-
Portuguese explorer João Vaz Corte-Real may have reached Canada.

-1492-
Christopher Columbus sails to the Bahamas for Spain.

-1524-
Giovanni da Verrazzano sails to Canada for France, possibly with Cartier onboard.

Early Life of Cartier

Jacques Cartier was born in the seaport town of St. Malo, France. Historians know very little about Cartier's childhood and early life. They believe that his father and uncles were probably sailors who taught him how to sail, navigate, and oversee a ship at a young age.

Getting Sea Legs

When Cartier was a young man, the fishermen of St. Malo made regular trips across the Atlantic Ocean to fish for cod in the waters around present-day Newfoundland. Historians believe that Cartier probably went on some of these voyages, where he learned the basics of sea navigation. Some historians believe that he went on expeditions to Newfoundland and Brazil in 1524, and possibly again in 1527, with explorer Giovanni da Verrazzano. By the time Cartier led his first expedition, he had been on enough voyages to be considered an experienced sailor and master navigator.

(left) Codfish were plentiful off the east coast of present-day Newfoundland, and this made it a popular spot for French fishing boats by the end of the 1400s.

Competition for Colonies

Portugal's Prince Henry promoted Portuguese sea expeditions in the mid-1400s. By the end of the 1400s, the Portuguese had built colonies in the Far East, giving them access to a wealth of trade goods. On the other side of the globe, explorer Christopher Columbus proved that there were opportunities for trade and colonization in the New World. European kings and queens began funding voyages to explore and claim new territory.

France's Bid for the New World

The king of France, Francois I, sent Jacques Cartier on his first voyage for two reasons. He hoped that finding the Northwest Passage to Asia would give France access to trade goods, such as silk and spices. He also hoped Cartier would find gold and other riches in the New World, which would bring wealth to France and help it regain its position as a strong European nation. Any information that Cartier could bring back about the geography, inhabitants, and resources of the New World would be useful for later expeditions.

(background) St. Malo, France, was a seaport town filled with sailors, traders, and fishermen.

(right) King Francois was eager to advance trade and claim territory overseas. France was in debt after waging wars against Italy for 40 years. The king had also invested money in large, costly palaces and public buildings.

The Northwest Passage

In 1534, King Francois hired Cartier to lead an expedition to look for the Northwest Passage. The king gave Cartier money for two ships, a crew of sixty-one men, and supplies for the journey. Cartier and his crew left France and crossed the Atlantic Ocean in less than three weeks.

Newfoundland Beginnings

The expedition arrived at Cape Bonavista, off the east coast of present-day Newfoundland. The crew spent a month exploring the coast, including an island that Cartier called *Isle des Oiseaux*, or Island of Birds. This is now known as Funk Island. Cartier's crew hunted sea birds and salted the meat to preserve it. They headed north up the coast and around the top of Newfoundland, passing what later became Bell Island. They sailed through the Strait of Belle Isle, between the mainland and the northwest coast of Newfoundland, and anchored on the mainland at Brest, a French fishing port. Brest is now called *Vieux-Port*, or Old Fort, and is in the province of Quebec, Canada.

New Lands, New Acquaintances

In Brest, Cartier and his crew explored the coastline using their longboats, or large rowboats. The coastline was rocky and barren. The crew continued south, crossing a waterway that is now known as the Gulf of St. Lawrence. They landed on an island that Cartier called Brion Island. It is now known as Prince Edward Island. Cartier's crew spotted some Native peoples on the shore, who quickly disappeared. Historians believe that these were probably Beothuk peoples, a Native group that no longer exists today.

(left) Funk Island was completely covered in birds, including great auks, which are now extinct.

Meeting the Mi'kmaq Peoples

Cartier's ships continued north up the coast of present-day New Brunswick and past the bay that Cartier named *Baie de Chaleur*, or the Bay of Heat. They anchored at a cove they named St. Martin's Cove, and explored the shoreline in their longboats. They encountered a **flotilla** of 50 canoes paddled by Native peoples. Historians believe that this group probably belonged to the Mi'kmaq nation. The Mi'kmaq were fishing for food and meant the Europeans no harm, but Cartier and his crew were frightened because they were outnumbered. The French fired their **muskets** over the heads of the Mi'kmaq peoples to frighten them away. The next day, Cartier's crew went ashore to meet the Mi'kmaq peoples. The French traded knives and iron tools in exchange for furs. They communicated with each other through hand gestures.

(background) A painting of Cartier's expedition exploring the St. Lawrence River.

-April 20, 1534-
Cartier leaves
St. Malo.

-May 10, 1534-
Cartier arrives at
Cape Bonavista.

-July 25, 1534-
Cartier leaves
Gaspé Bay with
Domagaya and
Taignoagny, two
Native peoples.

-September 5,
1534-
Cartier arrives in
St. Malo, after a
stormy crossing
of the Atlantic.

Meeting the St. Lawrence Iroquois

Cartier's crew traveled north toward what was later named the Gaspé Peninsula. They explored the coastline for a week until a fierce storm drove them to shelter in Gaspé Bay. They met some Native peoples while anchored there. Historians are not sure which nation these peoples belonged to, but they are referred to as the St. Lawrence Iroquois because they spoke the Laurentian **dialect** of the Iroquoian language, and lived near the St. Lawrence River. The Iroquois peoples were also known as the Haudenosaunee.

Crossing the Line

Before leaving Gaspé Bay, Cartier built a wooden cross on the shore at the mouth of the bay. With this he laid claim to the land in the name of France. The chief of the local peoples, Donnacona, became suspicious of the landmark and confronted Cartier, who explained that the cross was meant to mark the entrance of the bay so he could return to the same place on his next voyage. Cartier asked Donnacona to allow his sons to come back to France with him, so they could learn the French language and act as **interpreters** and **guides** on his next voyages. Historians disagree about whether Donnacona's sons, Domagaya and Taignoagny, came willingly, or if Cartier kidnapped them. Either way, the two young men left with Cartier the next day.

Cartier and his crew traded knives and other goods for furs from the St. Lawrence Iroquois.

Journey's End

Before departing for France, Cartier went northeast, to an island he later named Assumption Island, between the shores of Quebec and New Brunswick. The island is now known as Anticosti Island. Cartier stopped at the southeastern tip of the island, at present-day Heath Point, which he named *Cap de Louis*. The crew explored the island's coast for several days, but before they could sail all the way around it, storms blew in. Cartier was disappointed that he had not found the Northwest Passage, but he decided that it was too late in the season to go any further and returned to France.

(background) Cartier erected a cross on the shore of Gaspé Bay, with a sign that said Vive le Roi de France, *or Long Live the King of France.*

Foundation for Fame

King Francois was pleased with Cartier's expedition, and hired him for a second expedition almost immediately upon his return. The king gave Cartier three ships, money to hire a crew, and funds for one-year's worth of food and other supplies.

Familiar Territory

Cartier's fleet left St. Malo in the spring of 1535. The ships were separated in a storm, but reunited at a French fishing port called Blanc Sablon on the Quebec coast. Cartier made careful maps of the eastern coastline. Domagaya and Taignoagny recognized the area, and explained that the ships were close to the place where they had all met the year before. They also said that they were close to two territories, Saguenay and Stadacona. Domagaya's and Taignoagny's people lived at the Stadacona settlement.

The Gulf of St. Lawrence

The ships sailed to the Gaspé Peninsula. The interpreters said that a large river nearby led westward into the interior of the mainland. They called the river the Hochelaga River, but Cartier would rename it the St. Lawrence River when he explored it himself. The crew sailed along the western shore of the Gulf of St. Lawrence, north of the Gaspé Peninsula, and south of the shores of present-day Quebec. As the summer ended, they began looking for a place to stay for the winter.

(background) The waters of the Strait of Belle Isle were rough and Cartier risked shipwreck by sailing in them.

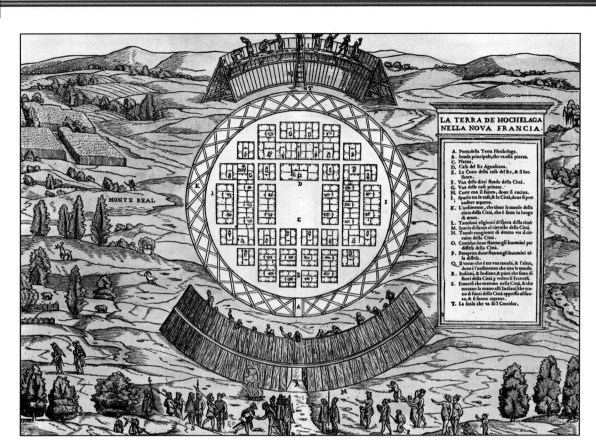

(above) Cartier and his crew built a fort on the banks of the St. Lawrence River.

Stadacona

Cartier and his crew sailed up the St. Lawrence River, past several small islands at the mouth and in the middle of the river. Cartier discovered Sept-Îles, as well as St. John Island, which is now called Bic Island. He also discovered *Ile aux Lievres*, or Hare Island, *Ile au Coudres*, or Coudres Island, and *Ile aux Bacchus*, now known as Isle of Orleans. Cartier and his crew set anchor at the Stadacona settlement, which later became Quebec City when the French colonized the region. Upon their arrival, the St. Lawrence Iroquois held a feast to celebrate the return of Domagaya and Taignoagny.

Tension

After the feast, Cartier instructed his crew to build a fort. He was worried about being attacked by the St. Lawrence Iroquois, so he told the crew to build the fort across the river from Stadacona. The fort was built where the St. Charles River now empties into the St. Lawrence River. Cartier wanted to continue exploring further along the St. Lawrence River, where there was another settlement called Hochelaga. According to Cartier's accounts, the people of Stadacona discouraged him from exploring further downriver, but Cartier insisted on going anyway. Hochelaga stood on the site that is now the city of Montreal, Canada.

Hochelaga

Cartier left the two larger ships **moored** near the fort and part of the crew stayed behind to guard them. He took the ship *L'Emerillon* and about 50 crew members to Hochelaga. At Hochelaga, the St. Lawrence Iroquois offered the French fish and corn bread to eat. The French gave the people axes and knives in return. The people of Hochelaga explained that there was a river close to their settlement, which flowed through a kingdom called Saguenay. They indicated that there were valuable metals at Saguenay, including silver and gold. Cartier went back to his fort encouraged by the news.

Winter Hardships

The winter was long and cold. The food supply ran out and many of the crew developed scurvy. Scurvy is a disease caused by a lack of vitamin C, which is found in fresh fruits and vegetables. Scurvy was common on long sea voyages, or during winters, when people ate only meat and bread. Scurvy caused black and blue marks on the skin, as well as swelling and pain in the arms and legs. The St. Lawrence Iroquois showed Cartier how to make a tea by boiling the bark and leaves of white spruce trees, which are rich in vitamin C. The recipe cured Cartier's crew within a week.

French Treachery

By the end of the winter, Cartier was ready to return to France but he was afraid that his crew would be attacked by the St. Lawrence Iroquois if they left. Historians do not know why Cartier was so concerned about being attacked, because the St. Lawrence Iroquois seem to have maintained peaceful relations with him and his crew. Cartier ordered his men to prepare the ships to leave in secret. He invited the St. Lawrence Iroquois to a large feast at his fort. When the guests arrived, Cartier invited Donnacona, Domagaya, Taignoagny, and some others to come aboard one of his ships, the *Grande Hermine*. When they did, Cartier took them prisoner. Cartier and his men departed for France with their hostages.

(background) Cartier surveys the landscape at Hochelaga, or present-day Montreal, Canada.

-May 19, 1535-
The fleet leaves St. Malo.

-July 7, 1535-
The *Grande Hermine* reaches the coast of Newfoundland. The crew waits at Blanc Sablon for the other two ships to arrive.

-August 15, 1535-
The fleet leaves Anticosti Island for the Gaspé shore.

-July 6, 1536-
The fleet returns to St. Malo.

The Quest for Riches

War between France and Spain delayed another voyage to the New World. In October, 1540, King Francois once again became eager to set up French colonies. By this time, Donnacona and all his people who had been kidnapped had died of illnesses in France, except for one young girl.

CANADA

Newfoundland

Atlantic Ocean

Sept-Îles •

Gulf of St. Lawrence

St. Lawrence River

Chaleur Bay

Quebec City (Stadacona) •

Charlesbourg Royal •

Montreal (Hochelaga) •

Jacques Cartier's 1534 route: ➤

Jacques Cartier's 1535-1536 route: ➤➤

Jacques Cartier's 1541-1542 route: ➤➤➤

Making Preparations

King Francois' main interest in 1540 was to claim more territory and bring the riches of Saguenay to France. The French did not realize that this kingdom was only a story that the St. Lawrence Iroquois had told them, and that the kingdom did not exist. Cartier was ordered to bring settlers to establish a French colony. The settlers were to farm crops, raise livestock, and trade for furs to send back to Europe, in an effort to bring wealth to France.

A Change of Heart

The king decided that the new colony needed a **governor**. He granted this responsibility to Jean Francois de la Roque, Sieur de Roberval, a high-ranking **noble**. King Francois made Roberval **lord** of any of the lands that France claimed in the New World. It seems that the king did this as a favor to his friend Roberval. Cartier was **demoted** from head of the expedition and was placed under Roberval's supervision.

(above) Cartier's ships depart St. Malo for a third expedition to the New World.

An Ominous Beginning

Cartier was given a lesser position for the third voyage, but he was still responsible for preparing the expedition. Cartier departed from France with 1,500 crew members and settlers aboard five ships. Roberval stayed behind to purchase and stock more ships for settling the French colony, and planned to meet up with Cartier in the New World. The ships became separated in storms on the Atlantic. By the time Cartier's ships arrived at the Strait of Belle Isle, they were low on supplies, especially fresh drinking water. Cartier and the settlers waited for two to three weeks for Roberval to arrive, but he never came.

Return to Stadacona

Cartier decided to sail on to Stadacona. He told the people that their chief had died in France. Cartier lied about the deaths of the other St. Lawrence Iroquois, including Domagaya and Taignoagny, and said that they had become powerful lords in France, and that they had not wanted to come back to Stadacona. The St. Lawrence Iroquois might not have believed this lie.

-1535 to 1538-
France and Spain at war over territory in Europe.

-1540-
King Francois hires Cartier for a third voyage to the New World. He chooses Roberval to lead the expedition rather than Cartier.

-May 23, 1541-
The expedition departs for the New World.

-August 23, 1541-
The ships
reach Stadacona.

-June 1542-
The ships at
Charlesbourg
Royal are
loaded and
leave the fort.

-October 1542-
The expedition
returns to
St. Malo.

Fort Charlesbourg Royal

Cartier and his crew sailed a few miles upriver from Stadacona to Cap-Rouge, where they built a fort named Charlesbourg Royal. They also planted vegetable gardens and started building a second fort on a high point overlooking the river. The crew found some crystals, which they believed were diamonds, as well as some metal **deposits,** which they thought were gold. Cartier sent two ships back to France to tell the king what they had done so far and to find out what had happened to Roberval.

Return to Hochelaga

Cartier had yet to find the kingdom of Saguenay, as King Francois had wished. Cartier decided to lead a small expedition up the St. Lawrence River, past Hochelaga, to see if a larger expedition was possible for the following spring. Cartier and his men traveled west for four days, eventually coming to a section of the river that is now known as the Lachine Rapids. When the river became too rough to travel by boat, the crew went by foot. They met several groups of Native peoples, who told Cartier and his crew that it was not possible to follow the river all the way to Saguenay because of the rapids.

(left and above) Cartier and his crew were convinced that they found diamonds and gold at Charlesbourg Royal. What they really found were minerals called quartz and pyrite, which were not nearly as valuable.

A Mysterious Winter

The French returned to Charlesbourg Royal, where the French settlement clung to life. Many settlers and crew members fell sick and died. Some historians believe that the settlement was attacked at this time. Cartier decided to abandon the fort and return to France.

Reunion with Roberval

In the spring, Cartier and the surviving crew and settlers loaded their ships to return to France. They stopped in Newfoundland, where they discovered Roberval and 200 settlers, who had begun building a fort there. Cartier thought that a French settlement was unwise, fearing an attack from the local Native peoples. Roberval did not agree and commanded Cartier to go back to Charlesbourg Royal. Cartier slipped away with all of his ships that night and returned to France without Roberval's permission.

(background) A small group of St. Lawrence Iroquois trying to stop Cartier and his crew from exploring the St. Lawrence past Hochelaga.

Life at Sea

Life aboard a sailing ship was often very difficult. The ships smelled terrible, were wet below decks, and were infested with rats and insects. The sailors lived in very crowded conditions and disease among the crew was common.

Grub's Up!

At the time of Cartier's voyages, there was no way to refrigerate food on ships, so the food often went bad or crawled with bugs. Meat and fish were preserved with salt. On calm seas, food was cooked over small fires on deck. Diseases like scurvy and **dysentery** were common because of the poor diet, and because it was difficult to find clean drinking water.

Discipline at Sea

Tempers onboard sometimes led the crew to **revolt** against their captain. For this reason, sea captains had to maintain authority at all times. Crew were punished harshly if they stole, fought, or disobeyed the captain's orders. Sailors who misbehaved were **flogged** with a whip or a knotted rope. They were also keel-hauled, which involved dragging a sailor underneath the ship from one side to the other using a piece of rope.

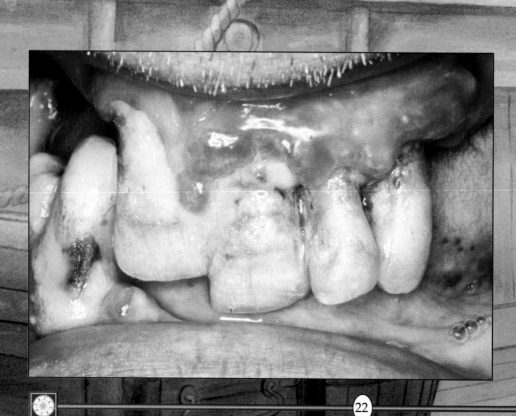

(left) Vitamin-rich fruits and vegetables were not readily available on long voyages, so many sailors developed scurvy. Scurvy was a painful disease that caused people's teeth to rot and fall out, and eventually led to death if untreated.

Crew Positions

There were many positions on Cartier's ships, and each crew member had different responsibilities. The ship's food and supplies were managed by the quartermaster. The boatswain looked after the sails and rigging, while the carpenter looked after the wooden parts of the ship, such as the **masts** and hull, ensuring that there were no leaks. Common sailors carried out the orders of the people in charge. For example, if the carpenter found a leak in the ship's hull, he assigned sailors to repair it.

(right) Crew members used basic tools to make minor repairs to ships during long voyages.

(below) Crew members added variety to their diets by fishing. They also ate local vegetables from the regions they explored.

Ogwissimanabo

In the New World, Cartier and his crew tried some of the foods that the local peoples ate. This simple recipe for yellow squash soup, called ogwissimanabo, is similar to one that Cartier and his crew might have made. Ask for an adult's help.

Ingredients:
1 medium yellow squash, diced
4 shallots with tops, chopped
4 cups (945 mL) water
2 tbsp (30 mL) real maple syrup

Directions:
1. Place the squash, shallots, water, and maple syrup into a large soup pot and simmer for 40 minutes.
2. Put everything into a blender and mix until it forms a thick paste.
3. Pour the mixture back into the soup pot and simmer for five minutes. Season with salt and pepper.

Aboard a Galleon

Historians know the most about Cartier's largest ship, the *Grande Hermine*. It was a type of ship called a galleon, which was a vessel commonly used for trade.

Galleons

Galleons had three to five masts and weighed from 100 to over 1,000 tons (91 to 907 tonnes). The sails were made of canvas, and were raised or lowered by complicated sets of ropes, called rigging, to make the ship go faster or slower. Topcastles were baskets at the top of each mast, where sailors climbed to watch for land, other ships, or bad weather.

Below Decks

Galleons had many different levels, called decks. The decks that were open to the air were called weather decks. The captain's cabin, the crew's quarters, and the gun deck were located below the weather decks. Large cannon were kept on the gun deck and were fired through windows called gun ports. Supplies were kept in **holds** below the gun deck.

Galleons were not fast, but they were sturdy. They were excellent ships for trade, because they could carry heavy cargoes.

Above Decks

The top decks were open to the air while the lower decks were inside the ship. The deck at the back end of the ship was called the poop deck. The poop deck was named after a Latin word, *puppis*, which means a raised back deck. It was the highest deck, so it had a good view for navigation and observing the crew. The quarter deck was a lower deck in front of the poop deck. The main, or spar, deck was a little lower than the quarter deck. The front of the ship was called the forecastle, and it was slightly higher than the main deck. Not all galleons had the same number of decks, since some were smaller than others.

Weather and Water

Ships during Cartier's time were made of wood planks that were fitted tightly together and waterproofed with tar. When weather conditions changed, sometimes the boards swelled or shrank, creating tiny gaps where water could get in. The shape, design, and sail rigging of each ship determined the ship's speed and maneuverability.

St. Lawrence Iroquois

Many different groups of Native peoples lived in the areas that Cartier explored. Cartier and his crew had the most interaction with the St. Lawrence Iroquois.

Villages and Fishing Camps

The St. Lawrence Iroquois lived along the St. Lawrence River, in the present-day cities of Quebec and Montreal, as well as along the Gaspé Peninsula. They lived in villages or fishing camps. Villages had up to 40 buildings called longhouses, where several families lived together. Villages accommodated up to 2,000 people, and were surrounded by protective walls made from tall wooden logs. In spring, summer, and early fall, people lived in fishing camps along the shore.

Language and Ancestry

The St. Lawrence Iroquois spoke Laurentian, a dialect of the Iroquoian language. This dialect no longer exists today. Historians know very little about the St. Lawrence Iroquois because they had abandoned their settlements by the time Cartier undertook his third voyage. The Laurentian dialect links the St. Lawrence Iroquois to many other Iroquoian-speaking groups, such as the Mohawk, Oneida, Onondaga, Cayuga, Seneca, and Tuscarora peoples. It is unclear what happened to the St. Lawrence Iroquois, but some historians believe that they were overpowered by their Huron enemies. Others believe that European illnesses wiped them out.

(left) The Iroquois were known for scalping their enemies, which led European artists to often portray them as violent.

(above and below) The St. Lawrence Iroquois grew corn and sunflowers for food.

Archaeologists *have found remains of Native villages along the St. Lawrence River, at the present-day cities of Cornwall and Prescott, in the province of Ontario, Canada.*

The Legend of Saguenay

Cartier and his crew first heard about the kingdom of Saguenay at the Hochelaga settlement. Since the kingdom was not real, historians believe that the St. Lawrence Iroquois made up the story so that the French would have a reason to leave and settle elsewhere. From Cartier's accounts, it seems that the St. Lawrence Iroquois were uneasy about the French coming onto their land and claiming territory. Historians cannot be sure of what the St. Lawrence Iroquois told the French about Saguenay, because the St. Lawrence Iroquois no longer exist, and they did not keep written records. According to Cartier, it was a land of untold riches.

After Cartier

Roberval stayed at the Charlesbourg Royal settlement after Cartier returned to France. The winter was very cold and many of the settlers became sick and died. Roberval could not maintain order over the settlement, and by spring, he gave up. Roberval packed up the ships and surviving settlers and returned to France.

A Discouraged King

King Francois was not eager to fund more voyages to the New World after Cartier failed to navigate the Northwest Passage or establish a French colony in the New World. The king was further discouraged because the colonists had failed to find the kingdom of Saguenay and its abundant riches. Cartier's "gold" and "diamonds" turned out to be worthless minerals known as pyrite, or "fool's gold," and quartz.

A Quiet Retirement

Cartier returned to St. Malo, France, after his third voyage. Historians do not know if he was punished when he arrived for having disobeyed Roberval's orders to return to Charlesbourg Royal. Cartier lived quietly in St. Malo until he died at the age of 66. St. Malo was suffering from an outbreak of a terrible disease known as the **Plague** at the time of Cartier's death, so many historians believe that he died from an **epidemic** of the disease.

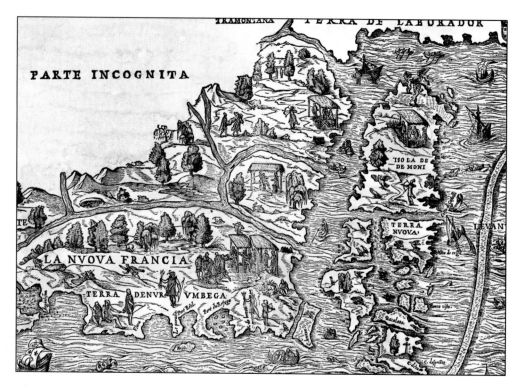

An early map showing the territory of New France, settled by later French explorer Samuel de Champlain. The map also shows part of the St. Lawrence River, first explored by Jacques Cartier.

The French Continue to Colonize

Sixty years passed before France sent another major expedition to the New World. Two trading posts were built in 1598 and 1600, at Sable Island, off the coast of Nova Scotia, and at Tadoussac, Quebec. Neither trading post succeeded because the settlers could not survive the harsh winters. In 1603, Samuel de Champlain followed Cartier's routes, exploring even more of the rivers and countryside. He eventually founded the colony of New France, which became a large French territory.

(background) Jacques Cartier is remembered in Place Jacques-Cartier, a bustling area in the heart of Old Montreal, Quebec.

-1603-
Samuel de Champlain makes his first voyage to North America.

-1608-
Champlain founds a French settlement called l'Habitation de Quebec, which later becomes Quebec City.

-1642-
Paul Chomedey de Maisonneuve leads the building of a settlement at the site of Hochelaga.

Cartier's Legacy

Cartier's voyages caused many changes in the regions he explored. The French settled the St. Lawrence River region, developing the fur trade and establishing farms. Thousands of Native peoples were forced out of their villages as a result.

Memorials

Several places in Canada honor Jacques Cartier. A major street in the Old Port district of Montreal is called Place Jacques-Cartier. The Jacques Cartier Bridge crosses the St. Lawrence River from Montreal to Longueuil, Quebec. It is the busiest bridge in Canada. The Jacques Cartier River runs through Jacques Cartier Provincial Park in the Laurentian Mountains in Quebec.

(background) A statue of Jacques Cartier stands at the explorer's birthplace of St. Malo, France.

Mixed Legacy

Many Native peoples do not celebrate Cartier's **legacy**. The Europeans brought diseases that wiped out entire Native communities. The Europeans had some **immunity** against these diseases, such as smallpox and influenza, because they had been rampant in Europe for hundreds of years. The Native peoples of North America had never been exposed to these diseases, so their bodies did not have any natural defense against them. As Europeans colonized North America, they took over Native lands. Small areas of land, called reservations, have been left to the Native peoples today.

(right) Cartier wrote and published a book about his experiences in North America.

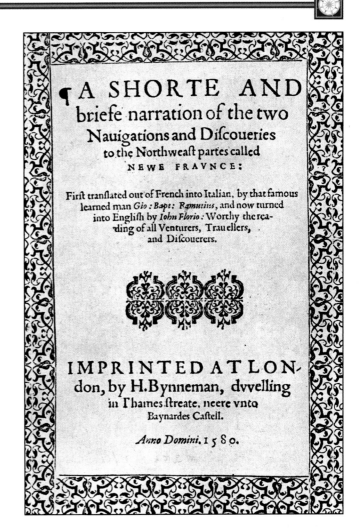

¶ A SHORTE AND briefe narration of the two Nauigations and Difcoueries to the Northweaft partes called NEWE FRAVNCE:

First tranflated out of French into Italian, by that famous learned man *Gio : Bapt: Ramutius*, and now turned into Englifh by *Iohn Florio*: Worthy the reading of all Venturers, Trauellers, and Difcouerers.

IMPRINTED AT LON-don, by H.Bynneman, dwelling in Thames ftreate, neere vnto Baynardes Caftell.

Anno Domini. 1580.

New France and the Fur Trade

Cartier's expeditions along the St. Lawrence River attracted other explorers to the region, and it was not long before Europeans discovered the healthy beaver populations there. At this time, beaver pelts were prized in Europe, and fur traders soon learned that they could make a fortune by selling the silky pelts overseas. Fur trading became the main business of the large French territory of New France.

(left) The lucrative *beaver trade became the foundation for the Hudson's Bay Company, the world's oldest merchant company.*

Glossary

archaeologist Someone who studies history by digging up tools, pottery, bones, and other items from the past

colony Territory that is ruled by another nation

demote To place someone in a position of less responsibility or authority

deposit A layer of a valuable material, such as gold, which is usually found underground

dialect A language that is specific to a region or a group of people

dysentery A painful disease that is caused by drinking unclean water, and causes terrible stomach pains and often leads to death

epidemic An unusually high occurrence of a disease in one region

expedition An often difficult voyage, usually in search of something, such as a place or route

Far East A term that describes a region in eastern Asia, including China and the Malay Archipelago

flog To beat, usually with a whip or stick

flotilla A fleet, or group, of boats

governor Someone who rules a territory on behalf of someone of higher authority, such as a king

guide Someone who is familiar with a specific region and helps others navigate their way through it, and usually communicates with the local peoples on behalf of the newcomers

hold A region below the weather decks of a ship, where ropes and other supplies are kept

immunity A body's natural defense or protection against disease

infested Overly populated, usually with a type of unwanted pest, such as lice or fleas

interpreter Someone who can translate a language for someone else or a group of people

legacy What someone leaves behind after death

lord A man of high rank

lucrative To make a lot of profit, or money

maneuverability The ease with which something can be moved or steered

mast Vertical poles that support sails on a ship

merchant Someone who buys and sells trade goods

moor To tie a ship in place so it does not float away

musket An early rifle

navigate To find or direct a route, often by sea

New World North, South, and Central America, as well as the Caribbean Islands

noble Someone who is born into a high class and is usually associated with royalty

Plague A terrible disease spread by fleas that live on rats

revolt To rebel or protest, usually violently, against someone or a group of people

Index

1 2 3 4 5 6 7 8 9 0 Printed in the U.S.A. 5 4 3 2 1 0 9 8 7 6